Windmill De Kat

Written by Hyo-mi Park
Illustrated by Jin-hwa Kim
Edited by Joy Cowley

big & SMALL

I am a windmill that produces dye.
Cloth is colored with the dye I make.
Years ago, there were many windmills
like me that made dye. But now
I am the only one in the world.
People call me De Kat.

Windmills have huge grind stones inside them that can crush raw materials into fine powders. Windmills, like De Kat, that made dyes could grind plants, minerals, insects and even shellfish into powders that could be used to produce the dyes to color cloth. "De Kat" is Dutch for "the cat."

When I was first built in this place,
there were many other windmills working,
pumping out water into channels.
The land is lower than sea level,
so the water keeps coming in.

Some areas in the Netherlands are below sea level, so the Dutch built sea dykes and used windmills to pump out the water inside the dykes. They extended their land by filling the newly drained areas.

Wind is the windmill's friend, but it comes and goes.
When wind is in a good mood, our sails spin,
but when it is in a bad mood, it can break them.
People watch the winds, and when there is a storm,
they open covers on our sails which protect them.

Thanks to hardworking windmills,
the Netherlands has become a fertile land.
Grass grows, tulips and roses bloom,
sheep and cows graze on green fields,
and people make all kinds of cheese.
Everything here is abundant,
and the cheese is shipped across the world.

The Netherlands is famous for high quality cheeses like Edam and Gouda.

9

Sometimes the country got flooded.
The river flowed over the dykes and into the village.
If the sails of windmills broke,
then there would be a problem with flooding.
But during wars, the dykes were blown up
to let some land get flooded,
stopping enemies from attacking.

One day, people brought machines to the village.
These machines pumped out the water,
and some windmills stopped working.
The machines had replaced us.

The windmill next to me broke into pieces.
We were all scared the same would happen to us.

But the rest of the windmills in our village
kept on working as we had before.
Only now we were not pumping water.
Some windmills milled mustard or flour.
Some windmills made paper from trees.
I spun my sails and made dye.

 There are now only 13 windmills in the Zaanse Schans village near the Zaan River, and De Kat is one of them. The windmills in the village produce paper, mustard, and dye.

The whole village was busy.
Ships came up the river
and took away cargo.
Our sails spun around and around,
and we were still the special beings
that the village needed for prosperity.

We were happy and had no idea
what would happen to us next.

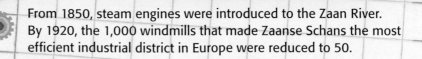

From 1850, steam engines were introduced to the Zaan River. By 1920, the 1,000 windmills that made Zaanse Schans the most efficient industrial district in Europe were reduced to 50.

Very soon, the world changed.
New machines took our jobs.
We no longer had to grind wheat
or produce paper from trees.
The windmills that no longer worked
broke down and began to rot.
My sails stopped as well.

Covered with dust, I looked at the Zaan River.
If I could have moved, I'd have got on a ship
and sailed away somewhere else.
My sails were broken, my roof destroyed.
Dust piled up in my body.

One day, some people came to see me.
They made a fuss about fixing me.
Carefully, they mended my sails.

Soon, my sails were spinning again.
I reached into the wind,
and the sky was beautiful again,
just as it had been in the old days.

The Zaanse Windmill Society was founded
in 1925 in order to restore and maintain the
windmills that still existed.

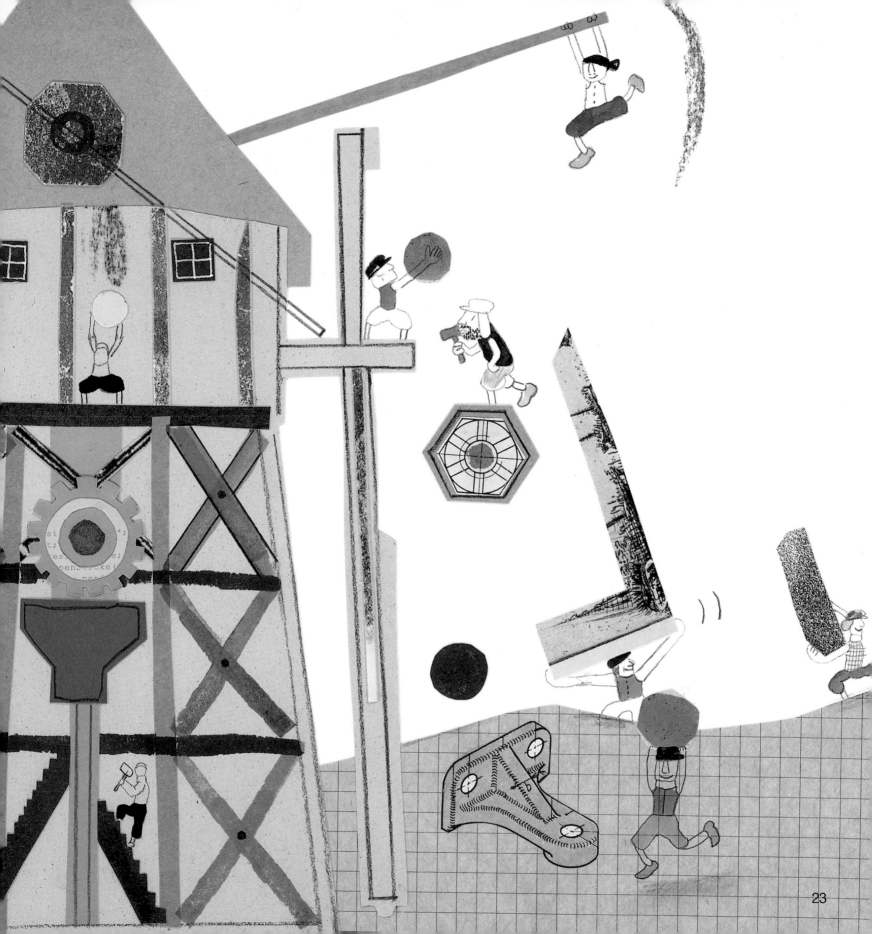

I am not as busy as I used to be.
At times I make dye for cloth,
but mostly I greet the people
who come to see an old windmill
that is still in working order.
The people look at my sails
while someone tells them
about the hundreds of windmills
that used to pump water off land
that was lower than the sea.

Sometimes, I miss those old days.

25

About the Netherlands
A Low-Lying Land

The Netherlands' flag is red, white, and blue. It is perhaps the oldest tricolor flag in continuous use. In the 16th century, the Netherlands was taken over by Spain. During this period, there were many independence movements, and people used this tricolor flag.

Living on Low Land

"Netherland" means "low land." More than half the country is lower than the sea so there have been many floods. People piled up embankments called "dykes" and pumped out water with windmills. The Dutch people struggled for over 1,000 years, fighting back the sea to extend their fertile land. These reclaimed lands are called "polder." As the polders stretched out, the map of the Netherlands changed.

Satellite image of a "polder" in the Netherlands

A Country of Windmills

The Netherlands was a country of windmills. Windmills were originally used to pump out water in countries like Turkey, and were later introduced to the Netherlands. At one time, there were more than 10,000 windmills used to pump water in low-lying areas. However, as steam engines and then electrical pumps were invented, the number of windmills decreased. Windmills were then used to grind wheat or make oil and dye. De Kat, the windmill in this story, is a dye-producing windmill in Zaanse Schans village.

Windmills in Zaanse Schans, the Netherlands

A Country of Tulips

The Netherlands is a country of tulips. The tulip was originally a native flower of Central Asia, but was introduced to the Netherlands in the late 1500s. Tulips became very popular in the Netherlands. People rushed to buy the rare tulip bulbs. The cost of one tulip bulb could be as expensive as a big house. The Dutch improved tulips, breeding many colors and shapes. Holland has 60 percent of the world's flower industry.

Keukenhof in Lisse, known as the Garden of Europe

A canal in Amsterdam

Amsterdam, a City of Canals

You can go anywhere in Amsterdam using the canal system. There are over 40 canals in the city, which is the capital of the Netherlands. There are more than 1,000 bridges over the canals. Small houses are packed closely together along the banks.

Once a World Trading Center

During the 1600s, the Dutch people traveled around the world by ship in order to do business. They sold tulips to other countries and purchased and resold rare items from Asia. They set foot in new lands – the explorer Abel Janszoon Tasman was the first European in New Zealand and Australia. It was also a Dutchman, Hendrik Hamel, who introduced Korea to Europe in a book called *The Journal of Hendrik Hamel.*

A picture of a harbor in the Netherlands in the 1600s

Rotterdam, Europe's Largest Port

Rotterdam is the Netherland's second most important city after Amsterdam. It is also Europe's biggest trading port. About 60 percent of goods arriving in Europe go through Rotterdam. Thousands of containers come in with goods from many nations. They are unpacked and then wrapped and transported to various places in Europe by trucks, trains, ships, and aircraft.

Goods are sent to various places via Rotterdam harbor.

Rational Thinkers

Most Dutch people think rationally and are very practical. They like to buy necessary products at a good price, rather than purchase luxury items that have little useful value. The "going Dutch" system of payment means when each person pays for themselves. Dutch people are keen on recycling and enjoy shopping at flea markets.

A flea market

Rembrandt's *The Night Watch* is a group portrait painted for the Amsterdam Civic Guard.

Pictures Capturing Ordinary Life

The wealthy people, who earned lots of money from trading or tulips, built houses next to canals and decorated them inside with beautiful paintings. During this time, European artists usually painted nobles or royals. However Dutch artists wanted to capture the lives of ordinary people, including the artist Rembrandt Harmenszoon van Rijn. Rembrandt lived an extraordinary life although he died early, and his technique and output was amazing. He is considered to be one of Europe's best artists.

Netherlands

Name: Kingdom of the Netherlands

Location: North-west Europe

Area: 16,040 mi^2 (41,543 km^2)

Capital: Amsterdam

Population: Approx. 16.8 million (2013)

Language: Dutch

Main religion: Catholic, Protestant (Christianity)

Main exports: Petroleum, natural gas, machinery, electronic equipment, transportation equipment, flowers, cheese

North Sea

*Windmill
An iconic part of the Dutch landscape

Leeuwarden

*Klompen
Traditional all-wooden clogs

Assen

*Alkmaar cheese market
A well-known traditional cheese market

*Amsterdam

*Royal Amsterdam Palace
The center of politics in the Netherlands for 200 years

Den Haag

*Tram
A self-powered street car

Enschede

Rotterdam

*Tulip
The Netherlands' national flower

Utrecht

*Erasmus Bridge
A bridge in Rotterdam – its nickname is "The Swan"

Breda

*Netherlands

Germany

Belgium

*Herring
Preserved young herrings with onion is a traditional food

Original Korean text by Hyo-mi Park
Illustrations by Jin-hwa Kim
Korean edition © Aram Publishing

This English edition published by big & SMALL in 2016
by arrangement with Aram Publishing
English text edited by Joy Cowley
English edition © big & SMALL 2016

Images by page no. - left to right, top to bottom
Page 26: public domain; Page 27: public domain; © Thomas Pusch (GFDL);
© kevinmcgill (CC-BY-SA-2.0); Page 28: all images public domain;
Page 29: © Erik1980 (GDFL); public domain

ISBN: 978-1-925247-27-5

Printed in USA